I Wonder

Karissa Jekel / Subi

Seeds of Faith

I wonder if the hairy caterpillar
knows it will become a
colourful butterfly someday...

I wonder if the tadpole
knows it will grow into
a hopping frog...

I wonder if this tiny sapling
knows it will one day be
a tall, tall tree…

I wonder if the baby swan
knows just how beautiful
it will be when it grows up…

I wonder if the stars
in the sky know just
how far their light
will shine…

I wonder how far
these dandelion seeds will blow...

I wonder how each snowflake gets to be
such an amazing shape and pattern…

I wonder if the snail knows
exactly where it needs to go...

I wonder if the sun knows
that it brings warmth and
light to our world…

I wonder if the rainbow knows
how much joy it brings us…

I wonder if the mountain sees
God's great majesty and glory…

I wonder if these kids know that

God has a special plan for
each of them…

I wonder what God
has in store for me!

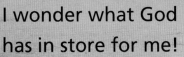

Activity

Make a Wonder Window

You will need:
- an 8.5 x 11 sheet of white paper, cut in 3 or 4 pieces
- a black pen or coloured markers
- 3 or 4 pieces of wax paper (these should be at least twice as wide and twice as tall as the 3 or 4 pieces of white paper)
- glue
- glitter or other decorations
- coloured construction paper

Step 1: Together think about some of the things you wonder about the world around you. Choose 3 or 4 of them to decorate.

Step 2: Write your wonders on a white piece of paper using a black pen or a coloured marker.

Step 3: Fold a piece of wax paper in half. Carefully cut along the top edge of the folded wax paper, rounding it to create an arched window shape.

Step 4: Open the wax paper and glue a wonder sentence face up on the right-hand side.

Step 5: Add spots of glue all around the wonder sentence and sprinkle glitter or other decorations there.

Step 6: Fold the wax paper closed and seal the edges tight with glue.

Step 7: Glue strips of construction paper around the 4 edges of the wax paper to create a frame for each window.

Step 8: Hang your creations in a sunny window or near a light to see your wonders sparkle.

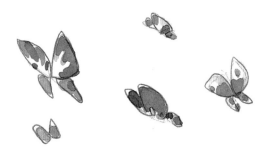

Prayer

Dear God,

May I always be in awe of all you have created.
Never let me forget that I am your creation,
made from the wonder of your love.
Amen.

When you search for me, you will find me,
when you seek me with all your heart.
Jeremiah 29:13

Originally published by Gemser Publications, Spain
Layout: Gemser Publications, S.L.
© Gemser Publications, S.L. 2011
El Castell, 38 08329 Teià (Barcelona, Spain)
www.mercedesros.com

This edition © 2012 Novalis Publishing Inc.
Cover design: Audrey Wells
Adaptation of text: Anne Louise Mahoney
Published by Novalis
www.novalis.ca

Novalis Publishing Office
10 Lower Spadina Avenue, Suite 400
Toronto, Ontario, Canada
M5V 2Z2

Head Office
4475 Frontenac Street
Montréal, Québec, Canada
H2H 2S2

Library and Archives Canada Cataloguing in Publication
        Jekel, Karissa
        I wonder / Karissa Jekel ; Subi, illustrator.

        (Seeds of faith)
        ISBN 978-2-89646-473-9

        1. Wonder--Juvenile literature. 2. Wonder--Religious aspects--Christianity--Juvenile
        literature. I. Subirana, Joan II. Title. III. Series: Jekel, Karissa. Seeds of faith.

        BV4870.J45 2012   j248.4   C2012-901221-1

Printed in China.

We acknowledge the financial support of the Government of Canada through the Canada Book
Fund for business development activities.

5 4 3 2 1   16   15   14   13   12